Arizona

BY MARI KESSELRING

The Child's World

Published by The Child's World®
1980 Lookout Drive • Mankato, MN 56003-1705
800-599-READ • www.childsworld.com

ACKNOWLEDGMENTS
The Child's World®: Mary Berendes, Publishing Director
The Design Lab: Design and production
Red Line Editorial: Editorial direction

PHOTO CREDITS: Clint Spencer's Photography/iStockphoto, cover, 1,
3; Matt Kania/Map Hero, Inc., 4, 5; David Liu/iStockphoto, 7; Richard
Walters/iStockphoto, 9; iStockphoto, 10; Kenneth Sponsler/iStockphoto, 11;
Arno Massee/iStockphoto, 13; Library of Congress, 15; Darla Hallmark/
Shutterstock, 17; Marcy Nighswander/AP Images, 19; Tomasz Szymanski/
iStockphoto, 21; One Mile Up, 22; Quarter-dollar coin image from the United
States Mint, 22

LIBRARY OF CONGRESS CATALOGING-IN-PUBLICATION DATA
Kesselring, Mari.
  Arizona / by Mari Kesselring.
     p. cm.
  Includes bibliographical references and index.
  ISBN 978-1-60253-447-6 (library bound : alk. paper)
  1. Arizona—Juvenile literature. I. Title.

F811.3.K47 2010
979.1—dc22

                                    2010016166

Printed in the United States of America in Mankato, Minnesota.
July 2010
F11538

On the cover:
The Grand
Canyon has rock
layers of different
sizes and colors.

CONTENTS

4 Geography

6 Cities

8 Land

10 Plants and Animals

12 People and Work

14 History

16 Ways of Life

18 Famous People

20 Famous Places

22 *State Symbols*

23 *Glossary*

24 *Further Information*

24 *Index*

Geography

Let's explore Arizona! Arizona is in the southwest part of the United States. It shares its southern border with Mexico.

NEVADA

UTAH

COLORADO

Kayenta •

Grand Canyon

Chinle •

Meadview •

NORTH

WEST   EAST

SOUTH

Colorado River

ARIZONA

• Flagstaff

CALIFORNIA

• Dewey-
Humboldt

NEW MEXICO

Wickenburg •

Phoenix • Scottsdale
⭐ • Mesa
• Tempe

Yuma •

• Tucson   • Willcox

•Tombstone

•Tubac

MEXICO

Cities

Phoenix is the capital of Arizona. It is the fifth-largest city in the United States. Mesa, Flagstaff, Tempe, Tucson, and Scottsdale are other well-known cities in the state.

Phoenix is named after an imaginary bird that dies in a fire. The bird is supposed to come back to life out of its own ashes.

Phoenix is close to low mountains. ▶

Land

Arizona has a lot of flat deserts. These areas are very dry and hot. Arizona also has tall mountains. The Colorado River runs along Arizona's western border.

Deserts and mountains make up the Arizona landscape. ▶

Plants and Animals

Many types of cactuses grow in Arizona. Cactuses are spiky plants. They do not need much water. The state flower is the saguaro (suh-WAH-ruh) cactus blossom. Arizona's state bird is the cactus wren. This type of bird often builds its nest on a cactus.

Saguaro cactus blossoms open in late spring and early summer. ▶

People and Work

About 6.5 million people live in Arizona. Many people work in factories. They make computer parts and other **technology** products. Mining is an important job in Arizona. Gold, silver, copper, and other **metals** are found in the land.

More than 60 percent of the copper in U.S. land is found in Arizona.

A dump truck works in a copper mine in Arizona. ▶

History

The first people to live in the Arizona area were Native Americans. In the 1600s, people from Spain explored the area. They claimed it for their country. Then the area became a part of Mexico. The United States bought the land from Mexico. Arizona became the forty-eighth state on February 14, 1912.

Members of the Hopi **tribe** had their photograph taken in the early 1900s. ▶

Arizona is home to many Native American tribes. These include the Navajo, the Hopi, and the Apache.

Ways of Life

Many people in Arizona are interested in the arts. Arizona is home to many writers, painters, and musicians. There are **influences** of Native American and Mexican **cultures** in the state. Different foods and art show this.

Native American art is sold in many places in Arizona. ▶

Famous People

John McCain is a senator from Arizona. In 2008, he ran for president of the United States but did not win the race. Sandra Day O'Connor grew up in Arizona. She was the first woman to become a U.S. Supreme Court **justice**.

Sandra Day O'Connor was a U.S. Supreme Court justice from 1981 to 2006. ▶

19

Famous Places

One of the most famous places in Arizona is the Grand **Canyon**. It is about one mile (1.6 km) deep. It ranges from 600 feet (183 m) to 18 miles (29 km) wide. The Grand Canyon has many rock shapes and colors to see. Many people visit this place each year.

The Colorado River runs through the Grand Canyon. ▶

Arizona is also called "the Grand Canyon State."

State Symbols

Seal

Arizona's state seal has the words "Ditat Deus." This means "God Enriches" in the Latin language. Go to childsworld.com/links for a link to Arizona's state Web site, where you can get a firsthand look at the state seal.

Flag

On Arizona's flag, the red and yellow stripes stand for the 13 original **colonies**.

Quarter

Arizona's state quarter shows the saguaro cactus. The quarter came out in 2008.

Glossary

ashes (ASH-ez): Ashes are the powder that is left after something burns. In stories, a phoenix grows out of ashes.

canyon (KAN-yun): A canyon is a deep valley that often has a river running through it. The Grand Canyon is in Arizona.

colonies (KOL-uh-neez): Colonies are areas of land that are newly settled and controlled by a government of another land. The stripes on Arizona's flag stand for the original 13 colonies.

cultures (KUL-churz): Cultures refer to the art and manners of groups of people. Arizona has Native American and Mexican cultures.

influences (IN-floo-unss-ez): Influences are things that affect other things. Native American culture influences the art found in Arizona.

justice (JUSS-tiss): A justice is a judge on the U.S. Supreme Court. Sandra Day O'Connor was a justice from Arizona.

metals (MET-ulz): Metals are hard, shiny materials such as copper, silver, and gold. Metals are found in Arizona land.

seal (SEEL): A seal is a symbol a state uses for government business. Arizona's state seal has the Latin words "Ditat Deus" on it.

symbols (SIM-bulz): Symbols are pictures or things that stand for something else. The state seal and flag are symbols for Arizona.

technology (tek-NAWL-uh-jee): Technology is scientific knowledge applied to practical things. People in Arizona make technology products.

tribe (TRYB): A tribe is a group of people who share ancestors and customs. The Hopi is one Native American tribe that lives in Arizona.

Further Information

Books

Gowan, Barbara. *G is for Grand Canyon: An Arizona Alphabet*. Chelsea, MI: Sleeping Bear Press, 2002.

Martin, Michael A. *Arizona: The Grand Canyon State*. Milwaukee, WI: World Almanac Library, 2002.

Minor, Wendell. *Grand Canyon: Exploring a Natural Wonder*. New York: Scholastic, 2000.

Web Sites

Visit our Web site for links about Arizona: *childsworld.com/links*

Note to Parents, Teachers, and Librarians: We routinely verify our Web links to make sure they are safe and active sites. So encourage your readers to check them out!

Index

arts, 16

capital, 6

Colorado River, 8

copper, 12

Grand Canyon, 20, 21

jobs, 12

McCain, John, 18

Mexico, 4, 14, 16

Native Americans, 14, 15, 16

O'Connor, Sandra Day, 18

population, 12

Spain, 14

state bird, 10

state flower, 10

tourism, 20